Langley Now and Then

Thelma Whiston

The Author

Thelma Whiston is a retired nurse who lives in Langley, Cheshire, with her husband David. Thelma lived in New Zealand for six years and Australia for twenty-eight years. Much of this time was spent in New South Wales with husband David and their three children Jane, Paul and Elissa.

Thelma's interest in local history started in the 1990s, when researching the Whiston family ancestors and their connection to the silk industry in Langley for her four grandchildren Karla, Tom, Pippa and Charlie.

First Published 2008 by

Langley Methodist Church
Main Road Langley
Nr. Macclesfield
Cheshire
SK11 0BU

ISBN 978-0-9545008-1-8

Printed by L & J Print Services Macclesfield 01625 669900

Contents

Acknowledgements

This booklet could not have been produced without the support and generosity of the people of Langley past and present.

I am especially indebted to Audrey O'Neill for the slides belonging to the late Cyril Dawson. Also to David Avery my sincere thanks for the Charles Tunnicliffe war painting found in the 1916 autograph book belonging to the Avery family of Canada. Special thanks, to Win Smith MBE for photos and papers relating to the Moore, Smith and Whiston families of Langley.

For his support, advice and critical appraisal my sincere thanks to David Bullock. His knowledge and up to date information has been especially appreciated in the chapters: Links, Methodist Ministers, and Church and Community.

Thank you to Alan Chapman for his expert guidance, advice and practical assistance in the layout of text and pictures in this booklet.

I would like to thank the following for their contributions of photos and items of historical interest: Mary Ashton, Norman Barber, Brenda Chapman, Barbara Cooper, Revd. E.W.L. (Taffy) Davies, Richard de Peyer, Jean Gosling, Ann Holland, Jean Jeffrey, Bill King, Barbara Knowles, Derek Lockett, Keith Mason, Marjory Morris, Lisa Noonan, Heather Potts, Audrey Smith, Dr Chris Studds, Mary Swindells, Margaret Taylor, Dora Wardle, Philip Wardle, Viv Warrington, and Andrew Wright.

I am very grateful for the assistance given to me by the following companies: United Utilities, Warrington, F. Harding (Macclesfield) Ltd., Adamley Textiles / David Evans & Co., Langley, Specialised Automobile Services, Langley, and the Macclesfield Museums Trust.

Lastly, my thanks to my husband David for word-processing my text and restoring many of the damaged photos and slides that have been used in the booklet. His constant support and encouragement has enabled me to finish this project.

Any mistakes or omissions are my responsibility.

Thelma Whiston 2008

Foreword

I was sent by the Methodist Church to work in Langley in 2004 and in preparation I made an initial visit to assess the lie of the land. At that point, I was given a copy of Thelma's first book 'A History of Methodism in Langley' which gave me an insight into the people and the place that I was to serve in. Although nothing could have prepared me for the reality! It really has been a wonderful experience.

Reading the way in which people interpret history is fascinating. Obviously there is only one truth about what has actually happened, however everyone has their own angle and interprets the situation differently. From these different slants we can build a fuller knowledge of past events. It is through reading the differing Gospel accounts of Matthew, Mark, Luke and John that we gain a deeper understanding of Jesus, the Christ. The Gospels are after all truly His-story! And ultimately so is this book, as we are His people and this is our story.

Through her own interpretation in this lovely little book (which I shall treasure), Thelma Whiston paints a beautiful picture of a truly wonderful place. This anniversary year will be my final year working with Langley Methodist Church. People move on and situations change, which is one reason why this book is so interesting, but we can always be assured of the faithfulness of God, His unconditional love, His never failing goodness. All of these things Langley Methodist Church has stood for, for 150 years, and for which it shall stand well after you and I are long gone.

I meet so many people who have a knowledge of God through reading about Him, and preconceptions about His Church, just as I had a 'head knowledge' about Langley without any experience of it. Actually coming to live and work here has been something else, something far richer, and more positive. This book will give you further insight into Langley, the village, the Church, its people, and the Lord, but I hope that you won't leave it there. Instead, I hope that this book will inspire you to engage with riches that Langley has to offer rather than leave it confined within its cover tucked away on a dusty shelf – I could tell you what an orange looks and tastes like, but until you have experienced it for yourself, you will never fully know; enjoy this book, but please do come back for more.

Finally, this book marks a very special and significant milestone in this corner of God's Kingdom; 150 years of worship in and mission from Langley Methodist Church – praise God for that! I really like the title, 'Langley Now and Then', all the photographs are great, each one telling its own story, and Thelma's text is very helpful and informative, yet all this raises an important question for me, "Now then Langley, what next?".

With my prayers for the church and community of Langley in exciting times to come…

Rev Stephen Dunn

Macclesfield

January 2008

Introduction

'A History of Methodism in Langley' was published in 2003 to celebrate the 300th anniversary of the birth in 1703 of John Wesley one of the founders of Methodism. Since then many changes have taken place in Langley both within the church and the local community.

To celebrate the 150th Anniversary of the present Chapel this booklet records some of the more significant developments that have occurred since 2003. It also includes recently received information about the church and the local community, including previously unknown anecdotes and photographs of bygone events.

'Langley Now And Then' is not a comprehensive history of Langley. It is a snapshot of some of the changes that have taken place over the years within the church and village, through words and pictures.

Langley Chapel and Cock Hall Lane, 1979.

Langley Past and Present

Situated on the southern edge of the Peak District National Park the picturesque village of Langley is the gateway to some spectacular countryside. The village lies in a valley overlooked by steep hills. Many streams come to the surface on their slopes and flow briskly towards and through Langley. Some of the water passes through the large reservoirs located in the valley to the east of the village.

Aerial view of Langley, c.1987.

The area is a nature lover's paradise with its abundance of trees, wild flowers, insects, mammals and birds, including a heronry. The nearby Macclesfield Forest is home to a herd of wild red deer.

Until the end of the 18th century Langley was mainly an agricultural community of tenant farmers who grazed sheep and cattle. Farmers supplemented their low annual incomes by selling wool, meat, eggs, butter, cheeses and milk at the weekly market in Macclesfield and other nearby towns.

The Bollin River flows through Langley and from the late 18th century attracted textile manufacturers and cotton bleachers to the village due mainly to the Bollin's exceptional quality of water and reliability of flow.

The Bollin River.

Robert Clowes, the owner of the Langley Hall Estate, built the first three mills in Langley between 1800 and 1805. They were originally named the Langley Mills and by 1830 called the Bollinhead Mills. Between 1820 and 1906 a further four mill sites were active.

In those early days the Bollinhead Mills were used by David Yates a silk throwster from Manchester and Isaac Smith a cotton bleacher and smallware manufacturer from Nottingham.

William Smith, a silk and calico hand-block printer and dyer from Manchester, established the Langley Print Works around 1820 in outbuildings near Langley Hall and by 1824 had built a mill on land close to Cock Hall Lane, where the business remained until 1964.

William Smith's grandson William Whiston inherited the firm in 1870. After 1870 the business prospered and grew, eventually becoming the largest silk printing, dyeing and finishing company in Britain.

The rare Queen Anne canopy over the doorway of Langley Hall, dated 1696.

The introduction of a very successful textile industry by these manufacturers changed Langley from a rural settlement into a thriving industrial community.

A block made in Langley for hand printing on silk and cotton.

Life at work and home, chapel and recreation, revolved around the demands and needs of the silk and cotton manufacturers. Many generations of Langley families worked in the mills over a period of 144 years. The closure of Brocklehurst Whiston Amalgamated (B.W.A.) (formerly Langley Print Works) in 1964 brought about many changes to the community of Langley. Skilled hand-block printers and screen printers became unemployed and many of their specialised skills were lost to the silk industry for all time. Some former employees of B.W.A joined the firm of Ernest Scragg & Sons Ltd., the textile machinery firm, who had purchased the B.W.A. site, others found jobs away from Langley and some moved from the village permanently.

Ward's Cottages at eastern end of Langley Playing Field and Bollinhead Mill (at right of picture) were both demolished in the early 1960s.

By 1845 an increase in the population of Macclesfield compelled the Corporation to seek a long-term solution for the supply of safe drinking water to the town residents. Two reservoirs, Bottoms and Ridgegate, were built to the east of Langley in 1850, Teggsnose Reservoir in 1870 and finally Trentabank in 1929. The first domestic supply of water in Langley was connected in 1895 to Ward's Cottages, Bollinhead Mill, and piped across to Clough House on Cock Hall Lane.

It was another seventeen years before all Langley residents were connected to the main water supply. Electricity arrived in Langley when Harold Whiston turned the power on at 9pm on the 26th April in 1928. Langley Print Works and cottages in Main Road were the first to be connected.

Main Road and Teggsnose from St. Dunstan Meadow (now Forest Drive), c.1958.

John Barber of Pyegreave Farm and his horse Toby on their milk round in Langley, c.1963.

The 1850 census records indicate that in Langley there were: a dressmaker; a milliner; a clog and patten-maker (patten, a wooden sole mounted on an iron ring); a butcher with slaughter-house; a blacksmith and farrier; two grocer shops, and the St Dunstan Inn. These businesses were supplying the everyday domestic needs of the villagers. By the end of the First World War many of the Langley shops had closed.

The introduction of a half-hourly bus service to Macclesfield in 1913 (fare 3d each way) and a wider range of cheaper goods in Macclesfield had altered the shopping habits of Langley villagers.

Outside Langley Chapel, 1913, the new Langley / Macclesfield / Broken Cross bus service.

Today the majority of villagers commute to Macclesfield or further afield for work, others work from home and a large number of residents are retired. Local children mainly attend primary school in Sutton and secondary schools in Macclesfield.

Children received a basic education of reading and writing as well as religious instruction when attending Sunday School at Langley Chapel. The Education Act of 1870 made education compulsory for all children between the ages of five and thirteen. To comply with the new Act a committee was formed in 1877 and plans drawn up for a school to be built in Main Road. The Langley Board School was officially opened in January 1878 and for ninety years local children attended the village school.

Langley Primary School, c.1970.

Last day at Langley Primary School before pupils transferred to Hollinhey Primary School, Sutton, 1970.

The school population of Langley increased greatly during the 1960's, and the Education Authority decided to build the new Hollinhey County Primary School at Sutton Lane Ends.

Langley School staff, 1970.
L to R: Joyce Dollimore, Freda Barber, Eileen Cookson, Mary Wardle, Mary Ashness, May Bayley, Margaret Taylor, Jean Gosling.

Hollinhey School teachers, 1970.
L/R, bk: Mr C Knowlson, Joyce Dollimore, Margaret Campbell-Kelly, Mr G Jones, ft: Margaret Taylor, Olive Llewellyn, Margaret Hay.

Hollinhey School opened in 1970 taking pupils from the former primary schools in Langley and Sutton. Langley School building is now a private dwelling.

The majority of dwellings in Langley were built between 1790 and 1870 and included three-storey weavers' cottages and long rows of terraced houses. The textile manufacturers and their families lived in modest detached houses close to their mills.

Weavers' cottages, Langley, built c.1800.

Employees and their families lived in houses owned by the Langley Print Works. At the end of World War One Harold Whiston, who had inherited the Print Works in 1915 from his father William Whiston, offered each employee the chance to buy the cottage they were renting. Very few took the opportunity of doing so at that time. At the end of the Second World War many tenants purchased the cottage they were living in.

View from Ward's Knob c.1967 showing building developments in Forest Drive and Teggsnose Mount.

New dwellings, Coalpit Lane, 1984.

The number of dwellings in Langley has increased over the past century, however the number of residents has grown only marginally during that period. In the 'good old days' the two-up and two-down cottages typically served as home for a married couple and their children, (census records indicate that five to seven children in a cottage was not uncommon). In recent times the trend has been for fewer occupants in each cottage.

Since 1924 small housing developments have been built at intervals on fields, allotments and former mill sites in the village, and in 2006 on part of the former B.W.A. Cock Hall Lane site.

Langley Hall Farm buildings, c 1980.

1984 development of the Hall Farm buildings as Whiston Mews.

Demolition of BWA's mill buildings on Cock Hall Lane, 2006.

Mill Fold development on the Cock Hall Lane site, 2007.

The closure of the village shop and post office in 1995 was a cause of much sadness to the community. The shop had always been used as a meeting place for villagers to have a chat and keep in touch with each other's needs. The closure led to the formation of the weekly 'Coffee and Chat' group held at Langley Chapel.

A shop and post office is open seven days a week in the village of Sutton Lane Ends.

Langley shop, c.1947.

Langley village, the Methodist Church and local industry continue to live comfortably together as they have done so during the past two hundred years.

Langley Chapel

From 1794, travelling Local Preachers held meetings for Methodists every Sunday in Langley village. In summer the meetings were held in the open air, and during winter months they were conducted in cottages or barns. By the early 1820s the local Methodists had grown in number. They and the Langley manufacturers supported the proposal to build a Chapel. The first Langley Chapel was opened on the 30th April 1826. This timber building served as the place of worship and education for the next thirty years. In 1856 a storm caused severe damage to the Chapel and it was later demolished.

The second Langley Chapel, c. 1890. This was built on the site of the first Langley Chapel 1826 – 1856.

Langley, which was growing in numbers, prosperity and confidence, was left with no place of worship, so the children of Isaac Smith and other local supporters began planning to raise funds to build a new Methodist Chapel.

A dedicated group of Langley Methodists organised many and varied fund raising activities as well as seeking support and donations from other Methodist congregations to build the second Chapel. After eighteen months the group had achieved their goal and the new Chapel was opened on the 21st May 1858, constructed at a cost of £1,350.

The opening of Langley Chapel one hundred and fifty years ago, after so many months of planning and hard work, was welcomed with enthusiastic celebrations by the Langley Methodists and Methodists from Bollington, Macclesfield and other nearby towns and villages.

Chapel members, c.1895.

There are only four graves in the Chapel grounds, making it one of the smallest graveyards in England. Some local Methodists have been buried in Sutton St. James' churchyard, and others in the Cemetery, adjacent to the Macclesfield Crematorium.

Elizabeth Pimm's 1870 gravestone.

Langley Chapel has been extended twice since it was built. In 1896 a two-storey extension and gable was built with a new external door and vestry. In 1911 the schoolroom was added and the foundation stone commemorates the coronation of King George V.

The 1911 extension, when new.

There have been other alterations, additions and renovations to both the inside and outside of the Chapel building including a new kitchen, toilets, gas-fired boiler, smoke alarms, roof repairs, painting, new gutters and downspouts.

A new Makin electric organ replaced the pipe organ in 1994 and in 1995 a new piano was purchased.

Inspecting the ceiling, during re-decoration of the worship area, in 1998.

Stained glass window in remembrance of Ann Prichard, d.1893.

One of the corbels decorating the main entrance carved in 1858 by Mr Richard Hassall, of Leek, a pupil of A.J. Pugin, architect of the House of Commons.

As with all buildings, the Chapel needs to be inspected constantly to ensure the fabric remains safe and secure.

In 1995 Heather Potts (then Heather Palmer) felt that there was an increasing need for some way in which loved ones could be remembered locally. The church had lost a higher number of members than normal in the previous year. The Property Committee with the approval of the Church Council devised a plan for the Garden of Remembrance, as we know it today.

Heather Potts (left), on duty, 2003, with Eileen Simons (seated), and Claude & Margaret Harlington.

In 1997 the Garden was created and in 1999 was dedicated by the Rev. Derrick Bannister, providing a calm, quiet oasis to the side of the Chapel, where garden seats are surrounded by shrubs and flowers and the memorial plaques of loved ones.

Dedication and Memorial Plaques.

To maintain the everyday needs of the Chapel and grounds requires a dedicated team of volunteers, who ensure that the Chapel building and gardens are well kept and maintained throughout the year.

Lawn maintenance? – go at it…

The Chapel is a warm, welcoming building for church members and the many others who make use of the spacious rooms and facilities.

Langley Methodist Chapel, 2007.

Leisure Activities

In "*the good old days*" some of the community used to participate in activities such as the baiting of badgers and bears and cock fighting. Others took part in bare knuckle fighting and wrestling.

Cock fighting is said to have taken place in the attic of Langley Hall in the late 18th century.

When the St Dunstan Inn opened in 1825 on Main Road, some of these popular 'activities' had been made illegal. The licence states '... *nor knowingly introduce, permit or suffer any bull, bear or badger baiting, cockfighting, or other such sport or amusement...*', and was signed by Hugh Roberts the first licence holder.

The St. Dunstan Inn, c.1970.

Country *sports* popular with men and boys in the Langley area were fox hunting, (between 1790 and 1810 a pack of hounds was kept near to Langley Hall), beagling, shooting, pigeon racing and fishing.

In 1841 the Langley Silk and Smallware Manufacturers formed a cricket club for men and boy employees who could afford a small annual fee. Such was the enthusiasm to join the club that it was possible to have two Langley teams. The owner of the Langley Print Works set aside a field for the use of the cricket teams near Clough House in Cock Hall Lane.

Langley cricket team, c.1899.

B.W.A. cricket team, 1933, winners of the Macclesfield Knock-out Competition.

After the closure of B.W.A (Langley Print Works) in 1964 the club continued to play on the old site until they moved to the present picturesque Cock Hall Lane site in 1975.

A clubhouse was built and cricket continues to be played every summer by members of the Langley Cricket Club.

Langley cricket match, 2007, on the Cock Hall Lane ground.

The Langley Rovers Football Club was formed in 1881 and played many local clubs with great success. They were taken over in 1904 by the Langley Sunday School Football Club. The team played many other amateur clubs until the onset of World War One when they disbanded. Competition football was later played in Langley from 1920 until the early 1990s.

Langley Sunday School Football Team, c.1920, on the Hollins field.

bk: _ Parrot, J Wardle, J Blackshaw, J Wardle, F Wardle, J Hammond.
ft: W Wood, J Noble, S Noble, H Rose, Cyril Dawson.

A 1970s football match, on the Langley Playing Field.

Angling was and still remains a popular pastime for young and old. Within walking and cycling distances of the village, enthusiasts are able to fish in the canals, ponds, streams and reservoirs. To fish in the reservoirs and some local ponds it is necessary to become a member of one of the three local angling clubs or societies.

Restocking Teggsnose Reservoir with carp, c.1970.

Before the *"modern era"* women were often too busy with domestic chores and looking after their families to participate in outdoor activities. Young girls were required to care for younger siblings and to assist with housekeeping duties. When they had some free time, they could play. Ball games, hopscotch, skipping and dancing were popular.

"Elbow grease", an undated photograph taken in Langley.

An annual Autumn Queen Fête commenced in 1971 organised by a group known as the Langley Mothers' Committee and held on the Hollins Field behind Langley Wood. The highlight of the fête was the crowning of the Autumn Queen, the first being Elizabeth Cusick (*neé* Oldfield).

The 1974 Autumn Queen, Eileen Avery.

Acrobats, 1971.

The All Girls Marching Team, 1973.

Touch down, 1973.

Dancing displays, acrobatics, sideshows and many stalls were popular with the crowds.

In the 1960s and 1970s the Langley employees of Ernest Scragg & Son and local villagers entered floats in the Macclesfield Carnival in competition with other local villages and employers.

The Langley Float, c.1970.

In 1990 a group of Langley residents organised the first Langley Fête to be held annually on the Playing Field behind Main Road.

This popular event has many varied displays, sideshows and activities including the popular duck race held on the River Bollin.

The Village Hall (The Institute) has been the venue for many recreational activities since it opened in 1883. The Langley Horticultural and Flower Society held its first exhibition in 1885. Many Langley residents entered with produce grown on allotments that they rented from the Langley Print Works.

Thelma Whiston arriving to open the 2001 Langley Fête.

Robert Chadwick (former post man) in his garden at 55 Langley Road, c.1960.

"The Three Blondes": Eleanor Buxton, Elizabeth Leech and Viv Warrington, performing in the 2006 Langley Review.

Competition bridge and whist drives have been played in the Hall, also billiards, table tennis, darts and bingo as well as keep fit classes. Langley has never lacked residents with musical interests and talents. Music, spanning the classics to jazz, and folk to popular, have all been performed at different times.

The Christmas Parties and entertainment are always well received by senior citizens from the village.

The very successful annual Langley Review is a showcase for local talent and brings in much needed income to maintain the Village Hall. In 2006 enough money was raised to build a disabled access for the Hall.

Bill King and Derek Hopper performing in the 2006 Langley Review.

Langley's "Double Decker". A dry-ash privy which served the needs of those living on both sides of the entry between Number 30 and Number 31, Main Road.

The Double-Decker privy, demolished c 1966.

Langley Print Works Band, 1930.

Langley Print Works Brass Band was formed in 1920 with twenty-seven players. The band became very popular not only in Langley but also in Macclesfield where they played regularly in many of the local parks during the summer months.

Every Christmas the band accompanied the Langley Church choir and church members as they sang carols around the village. The band also led the processions of ex-service men to Langley Chapel for the Remembrance Service on the 11th November each year. Some of the members formed a small dance band to play during social events held at Macclesfield Forest and Wildboarclough. The members disbanded after the declaration of war in September 1939.

The Playing Field was the initiative of Miss Edith Whiston who in 1938 donated the land to the village for the use of the children of Langley for all time. It was opened in 1952 equipped with swings, slides, and a climbing frame and has since been developed and enhanced in accordance with modern safety standards.

Official opening of the Playing Field, 1952.

Langley Sunday School Harriers, c.1899.

The Langley Sunday School Harriers Club was formed in 1896 and had its headquarters at Langley Chapel. The club competed with Harrier clubs from Macclesfield and other towns and villages until the onset of war in 1914.

The present annual Fun Run is supported by competitors from all over the county to raise funds for chosen charities.

It starts and finishes at Langley Chapel each November and includes events for children as well as those of more mature years.

Competitors in the Langley Fun Run 2006.

The closure of B.W.A. in 1964, the introduction of television, changing lifestyles, and the needs and priorities of individuals and families, led to the demise of many of the traditional sporting and recreational activities arranged by Langley villagers. With the exception of cricket, pool and table tennis, no sports teams presently represent Langley in any league competition.

Outside Langley shop, 1978.

Christine Bullock and Ambrose Broadhead, at Langley Hall, c.1960.

Langley Chapel is currently the venue for various leisure activities, they include Scottish dancing, sequence dancing, table tennis, yoga and physical exercises for the young and the elderly.

New Year's walk to Shutlingslow , 2005.

A walking group at Dimples Farm, Macclesfield Forest, 1965.

The most popular forms of activity these days are walking, jogging, horse riding, cycling, fishing and bird watching.

Methodist Ministers

Until 1899 Methodist Ministers and Local Preachers visited Langley twice on Sundays and held prayer meetings on a Monday evening. Ministers would hold special services for baptisms and marriages. An increasing congregation encouraged the Trustees of 1898 to make a request to the Macclesfield Wesleyan Circuit Meeting for a resident Minister in Langley.

Rev. W. B. Alcock, c.1900.

The application was granted and the first resident Minister in Langley was the Rev. W.B.Alcock who arrived in 1899. He lived with Mr and Mrs Samuel Bailey Simpson at Hall Cottages.

The Rev. Alcock, who had become much loved and respected by the Langley congregation, left the village at the end of 1901 to work as a missionary in South Africa.

Between 1899 and 2008 thirty-four different ministers have cared for the spiritual needs of the Langley congregation.

Pastor F. G. Crane on a visit in the late 1940s to the Hambleton family, at their farm "Hallecombes", Sutton.

Outside Langley Chapel, during the 1958 Centenary celebration. The group includes past Ministers and Church officers.

The first Langley manse was attached to "Invercraig", the house now called "Abbotsdale", and was used until 1915. After the death of Mrs Jane Smith in 1915, "Bollin House" became available and was used as the Langley manse until 1939. Ministers have since lived in Macclesfield and look after more than one church.

The first manse, attached to "Invercraig" (centre of picture), with the Print Works, centre-left.
View from The Hollins, 1910.

"Bollin House", 1910.

"Bollin House", 2007.

Rev. Derrick Bannister

Rev. Derrick & Audrey Bannister, c 2003.

In 1994 the Rev. Derrick Bannister, his wife Audrey, and their daughters Katy and Amy, arrived from Blackburn to look after Langley and Broken Cross churches. Over the years Derrick involved himself in every aspect of life in and around Langley and Broken Cross. His dedication, cheerfulness and sense of humour as well as his musical 'genius' on the accordion inspired Methodists and other denominations to join in and contribute to church life.

It was Derrick who, with the Revd. E.W.L. (*Taffy*) Davies, led the members of Langley Church and St James' Church, Sutton in a service of commemoration to celebrate the Anglican-Methodist Covenant in 2004.

Derrick felt there was a great need to have a paid Chaplain at the East Cheshire Hospice who would offer comfort and ministration when needed, and he was largely instrumental in arranging such an appointment in 2002 when the Rev. Stella Cole commenced in the role.

In the last months of Derrick's ministry at Langley we shared the pain and sadness of the death of his wife Audrey from cancer in April 2004. Derrick left Langley in August 2004 and moved to the Garstang Circuit, North Lancashire, to become Superintendent Minister.

Rev. Stephen Dunn

We welcomed the Rev. Stephen Dunn and his wife Sarah to Langley and Broken Cross in September 2004. The youngest minister in the circuit, Stephen had come straight from college which he said had its strengths and weaknesses, "I come with lots of passion, energy and excitement as well as a lot to learn".

Rev. Stephen & Sarah Dunn, 2007.

Since arriving in Macclesfield Stephen and Sarah have been blessed with two lovely daughters, Grace and Eve.

In June 2006 members of Langley Church supported Stephen at his ordination in Edinburgh as part of the 2006 Methodist Conference.

Since 2004 Stephen has worked closely with other churches in organising Christian events such as the 'Big Deal Weekend' held in July 2006 at West Park, Macclesfield which attracted large crowds of different denominations and also many people who do not usually attend a church.

Big Deal Weekend, 2006.

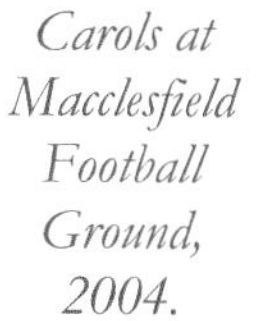

Carols at Macclesfield Football Ground, 2004.

Stephen stood in for three months as Chaplain to the Macclesfield Town Football Club in 2006 and at Christmas invited church members to participate in carol singing at the Football Club ground.

In 2006 he led a very successful Alpha Course (*Meaning of Life*) held at the Sutton Church Hall, jointly with Revd. 'Taffy' Davies. Stephen Dunn is also very involved with 'Churches Together in Macclesfield' and participates regularly in joint services with the members of Sutton St James and St Edward's churches.

Book Sunday, 2006.

Father Peter Cryan, 2006, of St. Edward's Church, Macclesfield.

Stephen with other church representatives welcomed Father Peter Cryan at his induction ceremony as priest of St Edward's Church, London Road, when he took over from Father Fred Robinson on his retirement in 2006.

Broken Cross and Langley Churches, New Year's walk, 2006.

... and part-way along the walk.

Stephen has taken part in the annual Langley Review for the over sixties in the Village Hall at Christmas time, and has performed with 'Taffy' Davies in the Sutton On Stage entertainment. He is Chaplain for the A.T.C. (Air Training Corps) in Macclesfield and a trustee for Just Drop In, a Churches Together sponsored youth information and advice centre in Macclesfield. He regularly visits the Wednesday morning Coffee and Chat group at the Chapel, often accompanied by his wife Sarah and their two daughters.

Church and Community

"Chapel" has been used historically to describe both the Methodist buildings and the people who worship in them. In this booklet we have tried to make a distinction between the "Chapel", as a building, and the "Church", those who worship in the Chapel and go out from it to serve in the Community.

Increasingly the Chapel premises are seen not just as a place of worship, but also as a service to the community, in terms of outside organisations using the Chapel premises for their activities. In addition Church members offer their time and energies in working in community activities taking place outside the Chapel premises.

Jamie Walker's Baptismal party, 2006.

Book Sunday, 2006.

Regular Sunday Services are held in the Chapel Worship Area at 10.30 am and 6.30 pm accompanied by the organist or pianist and choir and led by a Minister or Local Preacher. At different times of the year the services take the special form of Holy Communion (monthly), Covenant (1st Sunday of the calendar year), Easter, Harvest, Christmas and Parade Service with Sutton St James. Services aimed at the whole family are held once a month. Special services are held as required for Marriages, Baptisms and Funerals and also Reception into Membership.

Langley Choir, 2005.

Church members are involved in numerous organisations in the community including; Pensioners' Club, Rotary, Beekeepers, Just Drop In,

Cradle Concern, Gardening Group, Historical Society, Macclesfield Silk Museums, Hospice, Macclesfield Hospital, Football Club, Rossendale Trust.

Langley is represented at the Macclesfield Methodist Circuit Meeting held every six months, and two of our members, Alan Chapman and Tony Lewis, have recently served as Circuit Stewards.

Church members work together in many different groups including; Banner group, Choir, Music Group, Monthly Newsletter, Bible Study, Website, Flower Group, Sunday School / Club, Prayer Meetings, also committees for; mission, worship, youth work, budget, pastoral visitors, and property.

Andrew Spray, 2007.

Amy and Robbie at J Club, 2005.

Decisions regarding the life of the local Church are taken at six-monthly Church Council meetings. Between meetings, the actions are implemented by the Minister, together with the Church Stewards, Secretary and Treasurer and others with expertise of the matter in hand.

The outside organisations presently making regular use of the Chapel premises are; table tennis teams, yoga (Macclesfield College of Further Education), exercise classes (Age Concern and Hugh Mellmoth), sequence dancing (Harold and Gloria Lonyon), Scottish dancing (adults and children), bridge players, painting group (U3A), and band practice (C.Reynolds and others). Other lettings of the premises are for events such as; birthday parties, educational events and the annual Fun Run held in November. During 2007/8 the premises were used by Sutton Scouts and Guides while their new headquarters was being constructed.

Scottish Dancing, outside the Chapel, 1937.

Scottish Dancing, 2006.

Langley Church members take part in activities with other churches including: Churches Together in Macclesfield, and the Big Deal; Redeeming our Community (Moss Estate); Ecumenical Services and Prayer Meetings (with St. Edward's and Sutton St. James'); services are held with churches of other denominations for Week of Prayer for Christian Unity; the Women's World Day of Prayer and Remembrance Sunday.

The Banner Group, 2007.

After the Sunday morning service most of the congregation stay and enjoy a cup of tea or coffee and biscuits. This is a chance to develop friendships and to take up points of interest with the Minister or Local Preacher who led the service.

The Barber Shop Quartet entertains, 2007.

"Seaside Rock" Holiday Club, 2007, Langley Chapel School Room.

Church members assist annually with the house-to-house collection in Langley for Christian Aid and the annual flag days for NCH, the children's charity and the Rossendale Trust. 'Wells for Life' Faith Lunches have raised funds for the wells and local hospital in Lubwe, Zambia. Over recent years fund raising events have been organised by church members and held at the Chapel, raising large amounts of money for other charities. Events have included slide shows, organ concerts by John Bowdler an organist at The Tower Ballroom in Blackpool, and a concert by the Silk Brass Band from Macclesfield. In 2005 a large and enthusiastic audience attended the film 'So Well Remembered', starring Sir John Mills, shown in aid of the Rossendale Trust. Much of the film was shot in Macclesfield in the 1940s.

Slide Show at Book Launch, 2003.

Some of the other events that take place, often on an annual basis and supported by Church members, are; carols at the Macclesfield Football Club ground, the New Year walk up Shutlingslow, Safari meal, the Scarecrow competition and musical evenings with the Langley Choir and Friends.

Following the closure of the village shop in 1995, Mary Ashton a life long Methodist and member of the choir, felt that the village community needed somewhere to meet and chat on an informal basis and so the weekly 'Coffee and Chat' started.

Langley Shop decorated for Queen's Jubilee, 1977.

Held every Wednesday morning in the Chapel premises it is well attended by thirty to forty people from the villages of Langley, Sutton and Lyme Green, as well as by visitors from Macclesfield and occasionally greater distances.

John Barlow, Philip Wardle and Bill King at a Coffee and Chat morning, 2007.

Shirley Court and Brenda Chapman, 2007.

Mary Ashton, Marion Barlow, Pat Deegan and Dora Wardle at Coffee and Chat morning, 2007.

Mary McQuinn, organising floral decorations, 2007.

Members of Langley Church ensure that the fabric of their chapel is well maintained so that it will remain in a sound condition for future generations.

As well as being a resource centre for many community activities, an even stronger emphasis is given to making the Chapel a welcoming centre of worship.

in Langley Chapel, Christmas 2006.

Links

It is in the sphere of Christian Unity that John Wesley made his greatest contribution to the world of the future. In his famous sermon on the Catholic Spirit he made clear that

'Difference of opinions or modes of worship may prevent an entire external union yet they should not prevent a unity of love and co-operation in the Christian witness to the world. We may not think alike on any subject under the sun, for human nature reveals an infinite diversity of mind and heart, but, we can all love alike and it is in the sphere of perfect love that all the people can and should unite.'

The first service in which Langley Methodists and Sutton Anglicans worshipped together was in 1840, shortly after St James' Church was opened.

Between 1863 and 1880 the choirs of the Churches sang together at each other's Harvest Festivals and Easter Services.

Sutton St. James' Church, 1890.

Revd. Alan Stout, c.1969.

An important change took place in 1965, when the Rev. Wesley Penny, Methodist Minister and the Revd. Alan Stout of St. James' Church held the first of the regular united services combining congregations from Langley and Sutton St. James at various Christian events including Easter, Christmas and Harvest Festival. Through these links Methodists and Anglicans have been drawn closer together and have become more aware of the traditions and practices of each other's church.

Langley Methodist Chapel, c.1950.

For many years discussions had taken place at the highest level between Anglican and Methodist church leaders to achieve a unity of faith. On November 1st 2003, in the presence of Her Majesty the Queen, Anglicans and Methodists signed a Covenant.

AN ANGLICAN-METHODIST COVENANT

We, the Methodist Church of Great Britain and the Church of England, on the basis of our shared history, our full agreement in the apostolic faith, our shared theological understandings of the nature and mission of the Church and its ministry and oversight, and our agreement on the goal of full visible unity, as set out in the previous sections of our Common Statement, hereby make the following Covenant in the form of interdependent Affirmations and Commitments.

We do so both in a spirit of penitence for all that human sinfulness and narrowness of vision have contributed to our past divisions, believing that we have been impoverished through our separation and that our witness to the gospel has been weakened accordingly, and in a spirit of thanksgiving and joy for the convergence in faith and collaboration in mission that we have experienced in recent years.

Langley Church celebrated the unique event by inviting the congregation of Sutton St. James to join them for the annual Covenant Service which took place on Sunday 11th January 2004 led by Rev. Derrick Bannister and Revd. E.W.L. (Taffy) Davies.

Fr. Fred Robinson with Rev. Derrick Bannister, 2003.

From 1995 Father Fred Robinson led St Edward's Church in shared ecumenical prayer meetings, strengthening the bond between the Catholic, Anglican and Methodist Churches. His cheerful and outgoing personality had a positive effect on the St Edward's congregation and when he retired in August 2006, at the age of 75, he left a warm, friendly and thriving parish.

Father Peter Cryan was officially welcomed to St. Edward's Church in October 2006 by the Mayor and Mayoress of Macclesfield, Councillor Jim and Mrs Ina Crockett and St Edward's Church congregation. Father Cryan was also supported by his local ecumenical colleagues, the Rev. Stephen Dunn of Langley Church, Revd. David Mock, St. Barnabas' and St. Peter's Churches, Macclesfield and Revd. E.W.L. (Taffy) Davies, Sutton St. James Church.

Ecumenical Prayer Meeting, 2007, St Edward's Roman Catholic Church Community Room. L to R.: Peter Simons, Rev. Stephen Dunn, Christine Smith, Janet Parkinson , Revd. 'Taffy' Davies, Father Peter Cryan.

The Revd. 'Taffy' Davies joined his first parish in the south of England as a curate in 1979. After a varied career as a full time minister and then an artist and illustrator, he became vicar of Sutton St James in 1999.

Alpha Course, held at Sutton Church Hall, 2006.

He enjoys a close working relationship with the Rev. Stephen Dunn with shared church services and events during the year. It has become normal practice to involve each others church membership when organising events including;, Alpha course, parade services, Easter service and breakfast, carol service, fund-raising for the Lubwe mission (Zambia) and weekends away at Rydal Hall and Scargill. Taffy is a regular welcome visitor to the Coffee and Chat mornings at Langley Chapel.

Having fun, Rydal Hall, 2007.

Walking group, Rydal Hall, 2007.

The Revd. 'Taffy' Davies and Rev. Stephen Dunn continue to work together and have encouraged the congregations of St James' Church and Langley Chapel to become ever closer in Christian Unity.

Rev. Stephen Dunn, Revd. 'Taffy' Davies and Rev. Stephen Travis at Rydal Hall. 2007.

Industry

Langley Print Works

William Smith a printer and dyer from Manchester arrived in Langley in 1820.

He commenced hand-tying of silk and then dyeing it and hand block printing, in an old building close to Langley Hall. As his business became more successful William Smith moved to land near Cock Hall Lane, building a new mill, warehouses and a small reservoir.

After William's death in 1848, his son John Smith took over the Langley Print Works, leaving most of the every day management decisions to his nephew William Whiston.

Langley Print Works, in the 1960s.

On inheriting the firm in 1870 William Whiston diversified and expanded the business and by 1875 was exporting large quantities of hand printed silk and cotton to Africa, India and Burma. The firm became know as William Whiston and Son in 1900.

African and Burmese designs, block printed, 1873 [permission of Macclesfield Museum Trust].

In 1915 Harold Whiston took over the firm and introduced many innovations to Langley, including the use of synthetic dyes and screen-printing.

The amalgamation of William Whiston & Son and J&T Brocklehurst and three smaller silk firms took place in 1929. The company name became 'Brocklehurst Whiston Amalgamated Ltd', known as B.W.A., and for a number of years they were a successful and progressive silk business in throwing, printing and finishing.

Hand-block printers, Langley, c.1910.

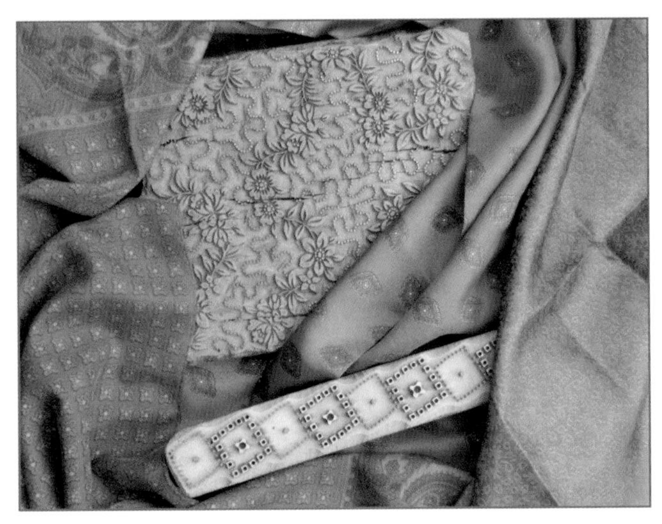

Hand blocks and silk prints, made in Langley.

After the Second World War the silk trade never returned to its pre-war output, having to compete with a less costly synthetic market and cheaper goods from overseas. B.W.A. Langley closed in 1964 and the site was sold. Tragically at least a quarter of a million hand-blocks were burnt on site and in the fire places of Langley cottages. A few were kept as souvenirs by local families and some were donated to various museums including Macclesfield Silk Museums. A large number were transferred to the firm of David Evans in Crayford, Kent in 1964 who continued to supply client orders.

The Macclesfield firm Ernest Scragg & Sons Ltd., founded in 1889, purchased the B.W.A. site following its closure in 1964. The firm designed and made textile machinery. Before moving to Langley, Scragg and Sons Ltd. were required by Macclesfield Borough Council to build a new entrance and road to the mill buildings from Langley Road facing the Hollins footpath. The new road would reduce the amount of heavy traffic to the village centre. Many alterations and extensions took place after the change of ownership: the 70ft. chimney was demolished, and many new buildings were erected to cater for the increasing overseas sales of textile machinery.

Scragg and Sons Ltd. built the widest single span roof of its era in Europe, c.1970.

Reiter Scragg, Langley, 1983.

Scraggs gained the Queens Award to Industry in 1969, 1970, 1974 and 1975. They continued to trade successfully until 1982 when in April of that year the Swiss firm 'Rieter A.G. of Winterthur' took full control of the business and continued to enjoy world leadership with its high speed texturing, uptwisting and crimping machines. By the 1990's the workforce of the renamed 'Rieter Scragg' in Langley was somewhere in the region of 600 men and women. However the local firm closed down in 2005 and its business was transferred to Switzerland.

F. Harding (Macclesfield) Ltd.

In 2006 part of the former Rieter-Scragg site was bought by F. Harding (Macclesfield) Ltd. Established in 1949 the firm is a successful yarn processor, specialising in all types of winding, twisting, doubling and heat setting of industrial and dyed yarns and sewing threads. Hardings process Polyester, Polyamide, Polypropylene and other speciality yarns. Some of the machinery that they are using was made by Scraggs. They have renovated and modernised many of the buildings on the site and have landscaped the grounds. The Company is wholly owned and managed by the Harding family, currently the third generation in the business.

Mill Fold

For the first time in 180 years part of the Cock Hall Lane site (formerly Langley Print Works / B.W.A. / Rieter-Scragg) has a change of use. Industry has made way for a residential development called Mill Fold. The mill buildings, including those built in 1826 by William Smith, were demolished in 2005. A partnership, between Dane Housing, Morris (builders), Macclesfield Borough Council and the Housing Corporation, developed the site and built 44 Affordable Homes for people who had a local family connection to Langley, Sutton or Lyme Green. The twenty-nine Shared Ownership Homes, together with fifteen Affordable for Rent Homes, became available in 2007.

Mill Fold opening ceremony, 2007.

The naming of the two roads in the housing development Whiston Close and Dawson Close are reminders of renowned people in Langley's past history. They are William Whiston, the former owner of Langley Print Works, and Cyril Dawson, the local historian, artist, author, nature lover and life-long member of Langley Methodist Church.

The Albert Mill

The Albert Mill, 1951.

For many years the Albert Mill, built around 1805, was water powered. The mill had various owners, and was eventually used as a screen store by Langley Print Works. The water wheel was sold as scrap in 1939 to assist the war effort. The abandoned mill building was demolished in 1952, and shortly afterwards numbers 14a and 14b Main Road were built on a part of the Albert Mill site.

River Mills
Built by William Frost of Macclesfield in 1906 as the modern Hollins Steam Laundry. Harold Whiston bought the building from William Frost's widow in 1918 and the mill was then used for many years as an extension to the silk finishing business of the Langley Print Works. Adamley Textiles Ltd., owned by Mr A. Adamski and Mr F. Parker, commenced a hand-block and screen-printing business in 1966. Thirty years later in 1996 Adamley Textiles Ltd. amalgamated with David Evans Ltd. of Crayford Kent. With an extensive archive of design pattern books the firm continue screen-printing, using modern technology to enhance the silk in the dyeing and finishing process. The firm produces high quality silk designs for this country and overseas markets.

Adamley's screen printing tables, Langley, c.2006.

The same source of particularly pure water that the pioneering hand-block silk printer William Smith relied upon in 1820 is still needed by the modern silkscreen printer today.

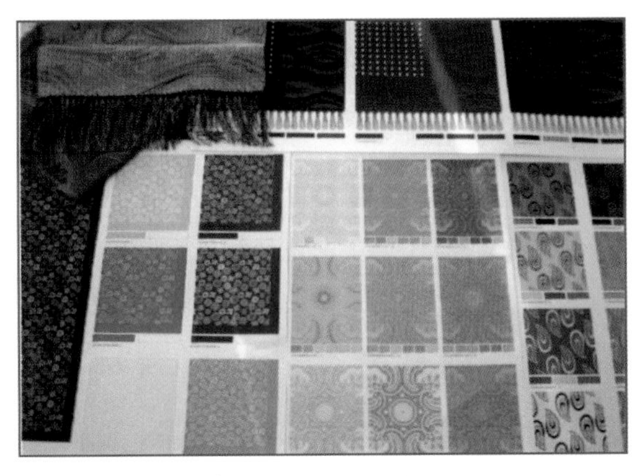

Some products and samples by Adamley / David Evans & Co.

Riverside Mills

Riverside Mills in the 1980s.

Built around 1837, Riverside Mills was extended by the Langley Print Works who used the buildings for many years as a silk finishing works. Dr Chris Studds purchased Riverside Mills in 2005 and is currently renovating the buildings to provide an educational centre, two cottages and a private dwelling. The educational centre will explore the history of the Silk Route through plants, a Persian Garden and the use of traditional dyes. Renovation of the mill pond, weir, race and water wheel, will supply renewable energy in a small hydroelectric scheme providing under floor, low voltage heating for the building.

The Bollinhead Mill and Warehouse

The Bollinhead Mill in Holehouse Lane, and the nearby warehouse, were built between 1800 and 1805. The mill was powered by a water wheel. Originally the mill was three stories high. For some years bindings, smallwares and tapes were produced in this building, and so it became well-known as the Tape Mill. In 1914 the mill was reduced to a single floor.

Bollinhead Mill when single-storey, c.1960.

In 1887 Mr John Thomas Moore commenced a furniture-making business in the Bollinhead Mill. He designed and manufactured adjustable chairs and tables. Some of the chairs were precursors of the deck chair. These were sold throughout England, until "JTM" retired in 1923.

J T Moore, in his chair workshop, probably about 1900.

From an early 1900's advertisement for John Thomas Moore's Langley made "Bar-Lock" chairs.

The Bollinhead Mill was demolished in 1967 and a private house, "Stag Hollow", was built on the site. In 1972 the derelict warehouse and cottage were replaced by a private dwelling named "Millbrook", now renamed "Pres du Doit".

The derelict warehouse and cottage in Holehouse Lane, c.1968.

"Stag Hollow", c 1970.

Langley Mill

Situated opposite the Village Hall and built in 1872 by William Hilton a smallware manufacture. After a variety of uses, Langley Manufacturing Company (Screens) Ltd. moved into the mill in 1964. They were commission engravers for the textile screen printing trade and made screen frames from both wood and tubular steel of all sizes, for customers throughout the British Isles.

Langley Mill, 1972.

Specialised Automobile Services

Working on a wire wheel, 2007.

Specialised Automobile Services makes and supplies a wide range of wheels, including "wire wheels", for vintage and veteran cars, with orders from all six continents. The current business, founded in 1980 by Steve Hopkins, transferred to Langley Mill in 1996. The use of the most up to date equipment allows this firm to produce nearly all components in-house. However, a great deal of the assembly is done by hand, requiring skill, time and effort and so only a small number of wheels can be produced daily. Steve Hopkins expects that with his specialist knowledge of everything car-related his firm will continue to produce high quality products.

Two eventful centuries have progressed since industry arrived in Langley. Although on a smaller scale, and more diverse than in the village's silk-based heyday, industry still plays an important role in the life of Langley.

Langley at War

The Victorian Empire began with the need to safeguard trade, and to acquire resources for trading. The growth of Britain's overseas empire led to many small wars in different parts of the world. But later wars such as the Boer War and the First World War helped to overtax the home economy which was already beginning to suffer from international competition, and would lead to an economic and social downturn for the country and its people.

John Smith, the owner of the Langley Print Works during the Crimean War, 1854-1856, set aside a field in Cock Hall Lane to be used as allotments by returning disabled soldiers. The allotments were later named the Crimean Gardens.

John Smith, c.1860.

The Crimean Gardens, in Cock Hall Lane, c.1970.

In 1855, to mark his safe return to Langley, Sgt. J. Wardle was presented with a gold watch and bible by John Smith at a celebratory afternoon tea, attended by Langley villagers and held in the first Langley Chapel.

For the Langley Print Works the First World War was to be most costly in terms of loss of manpower. The ninety-one Langley men who joined the services between 1914 and 1918 were all employees of the silk firm. The firm set up a pension scheme for the families of disabled servicemen and those killed.

The Roll of Honour for the ninety-one men who left Langley to fight in the 1914 –1918 War, including the twelve who made the supreme sacrifice, is in Langley Chapel's entrance porch.

Roll of Honour, 1919.

Many Langley and Sutton residents wrote in an autograph album compiled during 1916. Since WWI this album has been in the care of the Avery family of Halifax, Nova Scotia. Recently David Avery, of Macclesfield, visited his distant relatives in Canada. After returning, he wrote about two Langley brothers, Tom and Wilfred Avery –

> *"The brothers had emigrated to Canada, but returned to fight with the Canadian Rangers in the war. Before sailing for France both brothers visited Langley and Tom arranged for his wife to stay with relatives in the village.*
>
> *Tom's wife decided to compile an autograph album asking local people and children of Langley and Sutton schools to contribute. In the fields of Flanders in 1916 during a fierce battle the brothers became separated and during a lull in the fighting Wilfred came across a dead soldier and was horrified to discover that it was his brother."*

The verses, drawings and paintings in the album indicate something of the courage and sadness of the soldiers and their families. Amongst the people who contributed was the fourteen year old Charles Tunnicliffe who painted a patriotic scene. Charles later became a famous wildlife artist.

"The Lion and her Cubs", by C. F. Tunnicliffe, November 1916, painted on a page of the Avery autograph book [with permission of David Avery].

Harold Whiston presented the returned servicemen with gold medals in 1918 and organised two days of festivities for all Langley villagers including a day trip by train to Chester for all villagers over the age of sixteen.

The declaration of the Second World War was made in September 1939. The people of Langley must have felt a sense of shock and bewilderment, as experienced in the rest of the country. Those feelings were soon overtaken by a determination and resolve to contribute to the war effort. Many of the employees of B.W.A. joined the services, leaving a workforce reduced in manpower and skills. The Silk and Rayon Control, Ministry of Supply, was set up in Macclesfield under the Emergency Powers Act and was led by Mr O. Hambleton. The organisation arranged for silk to be transported to local mills for the use of throwsters, weavers, knitters and printers. B.W.A. produced items for the war effort including silk for parachutes.

Silk escape maps were printed and used by servicemen in Europe and the Far East. Government-inspired slogans such as the warning that "careless talk" can "cost lives" were also printed on silk in Langley.

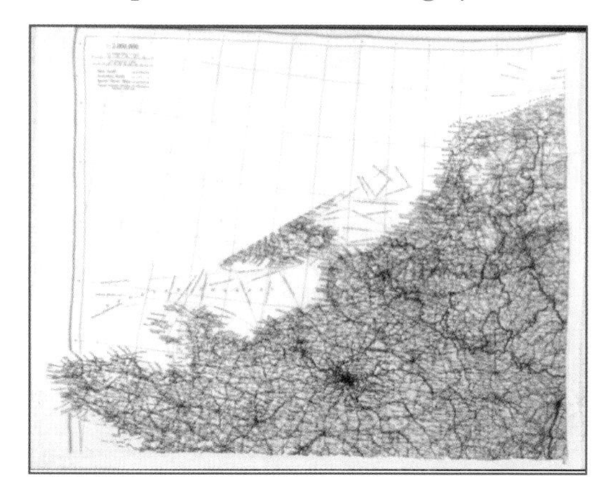

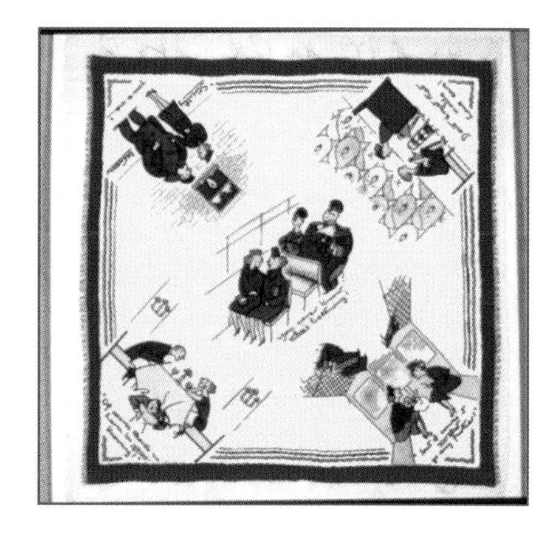

An escape map, and a warning against "Careless Talk", both printed on silk. c.1942,
[permission of Macclesfield Museum Trust].

Young men between the ages of 17-19 and men too old for the armed forces joined the Home Guard. They and the Civil Defence Wardens had their headquarters in the Village Hall. The Home Guard patrolled the reservoirs at night, with extra patrols during the day at Trentabank reservoir. These patrols ceased in 1943 and the Home Guard disbanded in December 1945.

Many events took place during the war years to raise funds for the 'Forces Comforts Fund', including weekly dances, concerts and the popular weekly Whist Drives, at which sometimes twenty tables or more would be filled in the village Hall. A total of 3721 postal orders and parcels were sent to service men and women during the war years and the Fund finally closed in October 1946.

A WWII poster.

Langley residents opened their hearts and their homes to the evacuees who arrived from Manchester and Liverpool in 1941, and from London in 1943. Some stayed just a few months and others for the duration of the war. Jean Gosling (*née* Bullock) recalled that the brothers Patrick and Dennis Barton, from Dagenham, Essex, stayed with her family at 24 Main Road, and how crowded her family's two-up two-down cottage became.

Audrey Smith (*née* Dale) lived at Doe Meadow Cottage next to Riverside Mills, where her father was the boiler-man for the mill. Their evacuee was Kenneth Walker from Liverpool. Many of the evacuees retained happy memories of their time in Langley. Jimmy Lofts, a Londoner, made a return visit. He said 'I love this place and the people are so nice, once you have been to Langley it draws you back again and again.'

Audrey Smith with Kenneth Walker, in Langley, during a return visit to the village by Mr Walker, c.1946.

During 1944 a number of Langley women worked part time for Vernons, a company from Liverpool owned by Mr Vernon Sangster. This vital war work took place in Langley Village Hall and involved packing thin strips of aluminium foil called 'Window spills' (or 'Angels' Hair' by the children of Occupied Europe). These strips were dropped from bombers to fool enemy radar operators into thinking that a large airborne force was approaching.

Mrs Barbara Hammond, mother of Mrs Barbara Knowles, is seated in centre of photo, with other Vernons' 'Outworkers', packing 'Window spills' in the Langley Village Hall, c.1944.

The announcement of VE Day (Victory in Europe) in May 1945 was an opportunity to celebrate. Servicemen and women returned home and were reunited with their families and loved ones.

The Roll of Honour for World War II for Langley and Sutton is on the War Memorial at Sutton Lane Ends, where the annual wreath laying ceremony is performed on Remembrance Sunday each November. The procession to the War Memorial starts from Sutton St James' Church following a united service with Langley Church, which is attended by the Scouts and Guides, members of the Parish Council and the Sutton Ex-Services Club.

WWII card, 1945.

Beautiful Countryside

Five hundred years ago Langley was part of the Royal Forest of Macclesfield, one of three hunting grounds in Cheshire used by the King and his court to hunt red deer, wild boar, otters, birds and other game.

The Teggsnose Country Park was established in 1979.

Vantage points on Teggsnose provide many varied vistas of the beautiful countryside surrounding Langley, and beyond.

A view from Teggsnose, 2005.

Over many years, small farms gradually encroached into the Forest as the tenant farmers felled trees for fuel and enlarged the grazing areas for their sheep and cattle. Grass, heather, bracken, gorse, bramble and bilberry grew in the clearings. Game animals became restricted to a smaller area of the changing landscape.

Rose hips.

Gorse.

Field boundaries were established with dry stone walls and hedgerows. Both these types of field-division had a variety of uses: they were intended to keep deer off the farmers' crops and grazing areas; to restrain the wandering instincts of farm animals, and also to act as legal boundaries concerning land ownership.

The walls and hedgerows provide shelter for small animals, birds, insects and plants.

Today dry stone walls and hedgerows surround most of the fields adding to the special character of the landscape. Modern fencing is also used, often to repair damaged sections of walls and hedgerows and also where enhanced security is required.

Section of a local dry stone wall.

Part of an old, local hedgerow.

Teggsnose Quarry, c.1910.

For many years, a short manually operated tramway was used to tip quarry spoil over the edge of Teggsnose .

Langley Chapel, 1940.

Architect's impression, c. 1838, for St. James' Church, Sutton.

Quarries existed on the summit and the slopes of Teggsnose from mediaeval times until recently. Much of the stone was an attractive pink and white sandstone. Teggsnose stone was used in public buildings locally, in Macclesfield and beyond. Stone from Teggsnose is in Sutton St. James Church and Langley Chapel.

In 1972 Brocklehurst Whiston Amalgamated (B.W.A.) sold a hunded acres of land (about 40-ha) to the Cheshire County Council. This area, which included the former quarry, is now known as Teggsnose Country Park.

Between 1979 and 1980 two and a half thousand trees were planted within the Country Park, and in 1980 a visitors centre and café was opened.

During summer months a herd of Longhorn cattle graze the slopes of Teggsnose Country Park: this rare breed herd belongs to the Bollin Valley Partnership. Wild flowers abound on the slopes of Teggsnose including the yellow mountain pansy, bluebells, tormentil and delicate harebells.

Looking towards Teggsnose from Bottoms Reservoir, 1970.

Bluebells & Mountain Pansies.

The Macclesfield Corporation constructed two reservoirs in 1850, Bottoms and Ridgegate, to serve the growing industrial and domestic needs of the population within Macclesfield. Teggsnose Reservoir was built in 1870 and Trentabank Reservoir was opened in 1929.

Teggsnose Reservoir, 1970, with Macclesfield Forest, planted in the 1930s, on the skyline.

Also in 1929 Macclesfield Corporation decided to establish an afforestation scheme adjacent to the Trentabank and Ridgegate reservoirs, to protect the natural water catchment area and also provide a source of income from the sale of timber.

Tree planting commenced in 1930 on a one-thousand acre (400-ha) site. The Macclesfield Forest contains three main species of trees, larch, pine and spruce. Smaller plantings are devoted to beech, ash, oak and poplar.

Macclesfield Forest is the main catchment area for the water that flows into Ridgegate and Trentabank reservoirs. The Forest is owned by United Utilities and managed by the Rangers service and has a visitors centre. The wide variety of trees, flowers and plants in the area are home to many animals,insects and birds. At least thirty types of fungi can be found in the forest, and mosses are well established in damp areas.

Wild red deer still dwell in Macclesfield Forest. These shy animals are rarely seen. Generally the only signs of their existence are their footprints in the mud and marks on trees where they have rubbed themselves on the bark.

A red deer stag.
[picture supplied by United Utilities].

At least twenty pairs of herons nest each year in the larch trees at the eastern end of Trentabank Reservoir. This is one of the largest nesting sites for herons in the Peak District.

A heron at the eastern end of Trentabank Reservoir,
[picture supplied by United Utilities].

"The Rooks"
painted in 1925
by Charles Tunnicliffe,
[with permission of the owner].

C. F. Tunnicliffe, R.A.

The artist Charles F. Tunnicliffe, 1901 – 1979, was born in Langley. Shortly after his birth he moved with his parents to Lane Ends Farm, Sutton. There, while he was still a child, he became inspired to draw and paint birds and animals that he observed on and around his parents' farm. The headmaster at St James' School, Sutton, Mr Buckley Moffatt, encouraged the young Charles to attend the Macclesfield School of Arts.

Charles Tunnicliffe later became one of this country's finest and best known bird artists.

Cyril H. Dawson

Cyril Dawson, 1906 –1999, lived in Langley for 93 years. He was a life-long member of Langley Methodist Church, and for many decades Cyril kept detailed records of Langley's industrial, social and natural history.

Cyril Dawson, on his 90th birthday, 1996.

Cyril was an amateur artist, photographer and author who is recognised as Langley's first local historian.

For many decades he observed the native birds, animals and plants. He shared his wide knowledge of the local fauna and flora with the readers of his column called "Nature Notes", printed in the "Macclesfield Express", for more than forty years.

In addition to natural history, Cyril also recorded aspects of local social history in a number of illustrated books that he published privately, all of which are now out of print.

The numerous public footpaths and bridleways that criss-cross the local countryside were well-used in the past by travellers, pack-horses, farm- and mill-workers.

"Leather's Smithy Inn", 2007, overlooking Ridgegate Reservoir.

These days, the paths, lanes and roads are often used for recreation: they provide access to Teggsnose Country Park and Macclesfield Forest. The local countryside is accessible for people of all ages and abilities who enjoy walking, cycling and horse riding.

Bibliography

Author	Title	Printer
Davies C S	History of Macclesfield	The University Press, Manchester. 1961
Dawson Cyril	Langley a History	Langley Teachers Centre. 1985
Dinnis Alan	St James Church, Sutton	Franklyn Press, Ltd. 1990
Smith Winifred	Franks Girl	Pentland Press Ltd. 1994
Sykas Philip A	The Secret Life of Textiles	Sandypress Ltd, Manchester. 2005
Whiston Harold	Langley	Times Printing Works, Macclesfield. 1947
Whiston Thelma	A History of Methodism in Langley	Franklyn Press Ltd. 2003

Sources

Adamley/David Evans & Co.	Langley
Alan J Chapman	Sutton
Archives of Langley Chapel	Langley
Cheshire Records Office	Chester
Macclesfield Harriers	Macclesfield
Macclesfield Library	Macclesfield
Macclesfield Museum Trust	Macclesfield
Macclesfield Scottish Country Dance Group	Macclesfield
Specialised Automobile Services	Langley
United Utilities	Warrington
Whiston Family Archives	Langley

Front cover main picture is of Bottoms Reservoir, Langley, looking towards Macclesfield Forest and was taken by Eric Whiston, 1964. The inset pictures are of the local bus in 1913 and 2007.

Back cover picture is of the entrance gate and sign at Langley Methodist Chapel and was taken by Alan J. Chapman 2007.